How To Maximize Profit Potential for Hubpages Projects

Penning Profits with Hubpages

How to Maximize Profit Potential on Hubpages Projects

by
Patti Markow

Disclaimer:

The author in no way guarantees that any particular amount of profits will be realized using the methods outlined in this book. The methods presented herein are simply the ways in which this author has found success, maximizing the profit potential on personal hubpages projects, and is hereby making the effort to share these methods with the reader. Individual success or failure of hubpages projects depends on the quality of work performed, along with the application of search engine optimization that is intended to drive organic traffic to published hubs, hence increasing the profit potential.

Contents:

1. Why Write?

Surely everyone has heard that there is money to be made using the internet and online resources. The world wide web is overloaded with schemes and scams of every kind imaginable. Most of these so-called profit producing programs are designed to lure innocent people into investing their time and money, promising the attainable achievement of some kind of financial independence. Most of them simply do not work.

Only after maxing out their credit cards do many realize that there is no easy way to make money online. At least, not the "make millions overnight" easy way to make money. If it were indeed THAT easy, everyone would be doing it and there would no longer be such a thing as a nine-to-five workforce. In order to realize profits from online endeavors, one must devote as much time and effort as is necessary to learn a new job and become good at it. There is a lot to learn.

When all is said and done, and hopefully not after too many of the schemes and scams have been tried, meeting failure, one must realize a particular fact that will always remain true: The overwhelming majority of people who use the internet are in search of information, not necessarily for something to buy. From this comes the saying that anyone who gets involved with money-making online is familiar with:

Content is King!

What is content? Content is all of the words on the internet, largely in the form of articles and the information made available on websites. There are approximately 25 billion or more pages of content currently indexed on the web. Someone had to write all of that content and, regardless of the amazing number of written pieces of work that are already existent, there will always be a demand for more. Sure, there is a lot of SPAM, such as a single article appearing exactly the same in many directories and on many sites, but godfather Google has been able to manage this by making these articles more or less obscure to an internet search user.

The demand is for innovative, unique work and the opportunity to publish such work is freely open to everyone. One need not even wrack their brain in order to write something that has never been written before. An author can research a subject on the internet and simply combine, in their own words, the information found on multiple sites. Then an innovative and new approach to that information can be incorporated into the work, making exactly the kind of written piece that Google, and the web searching public, should love. Such work, called "unique content," can be monetized, becoming a source of potential income for the author.

An author of unique content does not have to publish his work in his own name. There are numerous sites on the internet that hire writers who will ultimately be selling their rights to their work to others. Those others usually publish the work in their own name and monetize it with advertising and products for sale. However, the author usually ends up working for a mere pittance. Between the research, writing and the "cut" the broker site takes, an author can only make a one-time fee that equates to between $1 and $5 per hour. It is potentially more profitable for an author to take advantage of publishing platforms where he can publish and monetize his work in his own name. Through this method, there can be residual, passive income produced for the author for many years to come.

2. What is HubPages?

HubPages is one such publishing platform that anyone can join. HubPages is a free site and authors can publish an unlimited number of works, called "hubs," and earn money from advertising and products that can be promoted. HubPages offers tips and training and encourages involvement with the hub community through such as forums. All in all, it is a reputable, worthwhile site to become associated with.

Hubpages only permits the publishing of unique content. Videos, other media and images that accompany an article must be with permission granted and able to be used for commercial use.

Copyright infringement is not tolerated. HubPages recommendations for "acceptable work" can be found within the site's training center, but basically should be informative works and not be promotional of such as affiliate products or services. HubPages has a quality assessment process, during which each hub is manually reviewed for quality and compliance with terms prior to being published. If an author, called a "hubber," receives too many warnings or rejections related to his work, his account will be closed.

A new author can sign-up for his free account at:
http://tinyurl.com/yupperhub

3. How You Can Make Money with HubPages

HubPages allows for the monetization of each individual hub. One can earn income from advertisements that will appear on the hub and also from affiliate sales through Amazon and eBay. A hubber must qualify for a Google Adsense account before he can join the ad program and, likewise, must have an Amazon Associates account and qualify for an eBay affiliate account. A hubber will most probably not become rich from hub income, but some hubbers have reported that up to 30% or more of their household incomes are earned passively from HubPages.

4. **What to Write About?**

At HubPages you are permitted to write about almost anything, provided it is not illegal or otherwise offensive. What is recommended by almost all experts is that the subject of the web content one creates should be considered "evergreen" in order to be most successful. Evergreen subjects are subjects that have already stood the test of time. They are popular, the most searched for and, in all likelihood, will continue to be of interest to internet users for years and years to come.

There are three main niches that are truly evergreen:

- Health and Fitness/Weight Loss
- Love and Relationships/Dating
- Personal Finance/How to Make Money/Make Money Online

If an author writes about anything related to the above niches, his work will not become outdated as quickly as fad subjects or news stories. Hence, the word "evergreen" is used to describe such content.

There are a lot of sub-niches that can be thought of that are still related to the main evergreen niches, such as the use of fruit to make home-made beauty treatments, how to qualify for a home mortgage and birthday present ideas for a boyfriend. From these examples, one can see that there are many, many possibilities when it comes to finding something to write about.

Occasionally, a write will run into a "writer's block" and seem to be stymied when trying to think of a subject. There are several websites that offer assistance to writers who are in search of article ideas. One site is the Google Adwords Keyword tool. An author can simply type a general subject into the search term box and run a search of all of the related keywords. Examination of the resultant keywords can trigger ideas. If there are subjects of interest in the list of keywords that are returned, an author can do another search, and continue searching, by typing the subject(s) of interest into the search term box and running the tool.

Another site that offers title ideas to authors is ezinearticles.com. In order to take advantage of the title suggestion tool, one needs to sign up as an ezinearticles author. There is no charge for this. Once logged into his account, an author can click on the writing and editing tab. After navigating to the writing and editing platform of the website, in the left-hand column of the page one will see a link to proceed to the title suggestion tool. Possible titles can be searched by category and keywords. The titles suggested by the tool are, to the best of knowledge, subjects that ezinearticles authors have yet to write about, so it would be worthwhile considering these titles for use on a new work.

"How to" articles are usually well received and are popular on the internet. For suggestions of "how to"s that an author can pen there is a site called wikihow.com. At the wikihow site, there is a "how to" subject suggestion tool that anyone can use. No account is necessary. An author can search for subjects by category or even elect to utilize the random feature, where a random "how to" will be returned when the author clicks "surprise me."

5. **A HubPages Project**

A HubPages project can consist of one or more hubs. For the sake of this book, we will say that a complete Hubpages project is made up of three related hubs.

- Lead Hub
- 2 Supporting Hubs

The objective of the lead hub is to drive organic (search engine) traffic. It will target a primary keyword that offers the opportunity for the hub to rank in a preferred search result position. The lead hub will be optimized for the "rankable" primary keyword and also contain a YouTube video. The lead hub will be linked to the two supporting hubs.

When an internet user types a word or phrase into the search box, there can be millions of related pages that result. These pages are called "SERP"s (Search

Engine Result Pages). A preferred ranking position would be one of the ten possible listings that appear on the first page.

The two supporting hubs will be written on subjects that are related to the lead hub and their objective is to maximize income. They will target primary, high-cost keywords, according to Google Adwords. By high-cost it is meant that advertisers are paying the most money to target their advertisements to these particular keywords. The Google Adwords keyword tool will supply the information necessary for the selection of the primary keywords for the supporting hubs. The two supporting hubs will be linked to each other.

6. What is Search Engine Optimization?

One of the goals of a web content creator is to have his content rank in one of the top ten positions on the first page of search engine search results. In order to achieve this goal, content must be search engine optimized. Primarily, search engine optimization is done through the strategic use of keywords within the content. High search engine rankings can also be achieved through links back to the content page that are featured on other related pages, called "backlinks."

For the purpose of HubPages, search engine optimization does not have to be made into a major, complex project in itself. Writing the keyword-rich content and including the primary keyword in the article title, along with inclusion in at least one sub-heading, is basically all that is necessary. HubPages already has a Google page rank of 6, so that can work toward the hubber's advantage. YouTube has a page rank of 9, so embedding a video on the lead hub creates a high quality link for the hub, also working toward the hubber's advantage.

7. **Keyword Research**

Keyword research is a tedious, time-consuming task but it is an absolute necessity if an author wants to maximize the profit potential of his content. Narrowing down the primary keyword for the lead hub is the most difficult, demanding a decent amount of time and effort. In order to perform keyword research, one will need the following:

- Google Adwords Account
- Google SEOquake Browser Extension

To reap sizeable keyword lists and the related data, including the approximate CPC (cost per click) associated with the keywords and the adwords competitiveness of the keywords, one needs to open a free Google Adwords account. SEOquake is a free browser extension that will provide necessary data on the keyword competitors.

Note: Local Monthly Searches and "exact match" keywords are what pertain to the search engine optimization process.

First, the best keyword to target with the lead hub must be determined. Remember, the objective of the lead hub is to drive organic traffic, so what one must find is a keyword that is "rankable" that has the most local monthly searches possible.

- Log in to your Google Adwords Account
- The Keyword Research tool can be found linked to the "tools" tab
- In the search term box, type the subject of the lead hub (2 – 5 key words)
- Be sure "exact match" is selected in "match type" on the left side of the tool
- Select "advanced" options (optional). Indicate the country and language, then the number of local monthly searches >= the minimum monthly searches that will be acceptable. 500 to 1000 is a decent number of searches.
- The following columns should minimally be listed: local monthly searches, CPC.
- Sort the results by local monthly searches.
- Click "search."
- A list of possibly hundreds of related keywords will be returned, with the keywords that have the greatest number of monthly searches at the

top of the list.
- Google SEOquake should already be installed in the browser. Start at the top of the list. Click on one keyword at a time. (Only click on keywords for which you can create content. For example, a keyword like "mortgage calculators" is not a prime keyword to target with an article. The keyword should be a keyword for which you can write a article.) The option to do a search engine search of the keyword should appear. Choose that option. You may need to right click on the link in order to direct the search to open in a new tab.
- Examine the search engine result page (first page). SEOquake should indicate the page rank of the top competing pages. Of interest are basically the top four positions. If any page in one of the top four positions has a page rank greater than 2, you can basically forget being able to rank for that keyword and move on to the next keyword.
- Continue result page examination of the keyword list until a keyword is found where all of the top four competitors have page ranks of 2 or less.
- Write down the keyword found along with the local monthly searches and CPC data associated with the keyword.

There are certainly other aspects of the competing pages that can be considered when making the decision to target the keyword or not, such as the number of backlinks. Also to consider is whether or not the competing page has the keyword in its URL. Pages that include the keyword in the URL have a tendency to rank higher and are more difficult to out-rank.

There is a measure called "KEI" (keyword effectiveness index), which compares the number of monthly searches to the total number of search result pages (SERPs). If one were to take the time to compute the KEI for each keyword, the higher the KEI presumably the easier to rank for.

One can automate this search for a lead hub primary keyword using a tool that is available on the web. The tool examines the competing pages and the KEI, returning a rank difficulty measurement. The lower the rank difficulty measure, the easier it will be for new content to rank in a top position. The tool is called Keyword Project Manager. One can upload the entire Google Adwords keyword list (CSV format) and the tool can analyze the keywords, sorted by local monthly searches. At a glance, the researcher can locate a rankable keyword. The tool also has keyword filters in order to quickly narrow down the results. This tool has a 7 day, full-function free trial (no credit card required) and is very highly recommended. The tool frees up the time of the researcher to do other things while it comprehensively analyzes the keyword list. One can perform as much keyword analysis as desired within the 7 days and download the results for future reference.

One can sign-up for a Keyword Project Manager free trial at this URL:

http://tinyurl.com/yupperkpm

After the primary keyword for the lead hub has been selected, the next aspect of research that must be performed is the search for two related keywords that have a high CPC and are high in adwords competition. Search for these two keywords only requires a few minutes of time and one only needs the Google Adwords Keyword Tool.

- Log in to Google Adwords Account
- Go to the Keyword Tool
- Type the LEAD HUB PRIMARY KEYWORD in the search term box
- Be sure "exact match" is selected.
- Advanced search options are not necessary.
- Columns should be local monthly searches, CPC, competition.
- Results should be sorted by approximate CPC.
- Click "search."
- Starting at the top of the list (highest CPC keywords), select the first two keywords that meed the following criteria: are article friendly (good keywords for which an article can be written) and are HIGH

COMPETITION. The reason for high competition is that this indicates that advertisers are actually paying the estimated CPC for their ads, hence it is more likely that the content creator will be able to receive his share of the ad revenue.

- Write down the keywords along with the related data: local monthly searches, CPC.

At this point, the content creator is armed with three keywords. A primary keyword for the lead hub and two primary keywords for the supporting hubs. Three articles will need to be written, focusing on these keywords individually and in cross-reference. This is a good time to compute an estimated profit potential for the hub project.

To compute an estimated profit potential for the hub project, determine:

LMS (local monthly searches of primary keyword for the lead hub) x .20 (estimated share of organic traffic the hub will receive if it ranks on the first page of the search results) x .60 (hubber's share of impressions/traffic after HubPages takes their percentage) x CPC (estimated cost per click of one of the supporting hub primary keywords – the one with the highest CPC) x .05 (estimated percentage of traffic that will click on an ad) x .60 (ad revenue share to adsense account holder paid by Google) = Estimated Profit Potential for HubPages Project.

$$\text{LMS x .20 x .60 x CPC x .05 x .60} = \text{EPP}$$

8. Use of LSI (Latent Search Indexed) Keywords

One potential problem a content creator may stumble upon is keyword spamming. Although a primary keyword should be used to a specific density, over use of the primary keyword can work in a detrimental fashion, causing the content to be less worthy of ranking by Google. To avoid this potential dilemma, yet in order to emphasize the key subject of the content, LSI keywords are used. LSI keywords are not used in place of the primary keyword, they are used in addition to.

To find the related LSI keywords for any primary keyword, one need return to the Google Adwords keyword tool. In the search term box, type the primary keyword EXACTLY. Be sure "exact match" is selected for match type and have the results sorted by relevancy. The resultant keywords are all LSI keywords. One should select up to 10 LSI keywords for any given primary keyword. The criteria is only that the LSI keyword will be able to be incorporated easily into the article being written. Not all 10 of the LSI keywords need to be used. But at least five LSI keywords should be used for an article with a length of 500 words.

- Make 3 separate keyword lists
- At the top of each list, write one of the primary keywords for the 3 hubs
- Skip a line and write the 2 other primary keywords for the related hubs
- Skip another line and write a list of the 10 LSI keywords that can be included in the content.

9. Long-Tail Keywords

A long-tail keyword is a keyword phrase that contains four, five or more words. Many internet entrepreneurs have touted tremendous success using long-tails instead of the standard keywords provided by the Google Keyword Research tool. One of the primary benefits of using a long-tail keyword is that it will be easier to rank on the first page of the search results. There is also a down side to long-tails. Traffic can be dramatically lower than the use of standard keywords and Google does not maintain nor provide information, such as monthly searches, competition and estimated CPC, in its database. In effect, the long-tail user is basically using the keyword blind.

The suggestion of this author is to use long-tail keywords as primary keywords only in the event that standard keywords cannot be found that meet the analyzed, filtered criteria that is being used. For example, after analysis of many keywords and there is no keyword that is found where the competing pages have page ranks less than two, then perhaps one should consider using a long-tail keyword as the primary keyword.

To find a long-tail keyword, one need only type "how to" or "why" or something similar in front of the best primary keyword in the Google search bar. As one is typing, he will notice the Google auto-suggest feature is recommending additional words to complete the search phrase. That phrase that is being auto-suggested is a long-tail keyword that people have actually searched for, although exactly how many people cannot be determined. By playing with the auto-suggest feature, a suitable long-tail keyword will most likely be able to be found.

If taking advantage of the Keyword Project Manager's 7 day free trial, the software has a keyword research tool specifically designed to return long-tail keywords. This can significantly cut the time necessary to search for a long-tail keyword using Google auto-suggest.

Once again, Keyword Project Manager can be signed up for at this URL:

http://tinyurl.com/yupperkpm

10. **Keyword Project Manager Review**

Keyword Research Simplified with Keyword Project Manager

Keyword Project Manager is one all-around, top-notch keyword management and research tool. It is primarily designed to be used in conjunction with the Google Adwords Keyword Tool in order to find the best and most profitable keywords for an online project. Whether one is creating a website or composing an SEO article for web publication, Keyword Project Manager is a "must use" tool if one of the primary objectives is to effectively compete on the world wide web.

Some Key Features of Keyword Project Manager

- Analyze Keyword Competition
- Perform Supplementary Keyword Research for Long-Tails
- Keyword Management
- 12 Keyword Filters
- Easy Import of Unlimited Keywords from Google Keyword Tool

Keyword Competition Analysis

While most online entrepreneurs utilize the Google Adwords Keyword Tool to initially gather keywords and related data (global and local monthly searches, adwords competition, approximate CPC), there is more entailed in appropriately analyzing and narrowing down keywords. One must consider the page ranks of the top competitors, the KEI (Keyword

Effectiveness Index) and the SERPs (Search Engine Result Pages) when seeking the best keyword to use as a project focus. Keyword Project Manager automates the tedious and extremely time consuming work involved in analyzing all the keyword data.

Not only does Keyword Project Manager return the additional information necessary (page ranks of top 4 competitors, KEI and SERPs), Keyword Project Manager assigns a ranking difficulty score in order to more easily determine which keywords one would have the best chance of ranking in the top results for. The lower the ranking difficulty score, the more opportunity the keyword offers for a high rank in the search results.

If the keyword researcher is interested in the adsense profit potential for keywords, Keyword Project Manager computes that as well. The profit potential can be based on global monthly searches, local monthly searches or Google Search Network searches. The formula that Keyword Project Manager uses to calculate the profit potential is:

Searches x .4 (search traffic click through rate) x CPC x .25 (adsense payout percentage) x .05 (ad click rate)

Note: This reviewer found some possible flaws with the calculation. The numbers preferred by this reviewer are .2 (search traffic click through rate) and .60 (adsense payout percentage). 20% search traffic is a more conservative figure, provided the project ranks on the first page of the search results. 60% adsense payout percentage is more in line with what Google purports to payout when someone clicks on an ad. It has been experienced that the location of the person who clicks on an ad is also taken into consideration before Google computes how much to pay. However, all in all, the calculation used by Keyword Project Manager is only to provide guidance and basically balances out. It was reported by some users that Keyword Project Manager admin will adjust the formula for a specific user if that is specially requested. This fact has not been confirmed.

Search for Long-Tail Keywords

Keyword Project Manager provides the tools for a user to perform supplementary keyword research. A user can utilize these supplementary tools to determine long-tail keywords that are associated with Google and Amazon searches. The growing value of being able to locate related long-tail keywords is quickly becoming established.

Although the global and local search numbers take a dive when a long-tail keyword is used, the content creator's chance of ranking in the top positions in the search results skyrockets. When certain groups of keywords return results that show little hope of ranking in the top 10, opting for less traffic, but a high ranking, by taking advantage of a long-tail keyword would be the appropriate decision to make, insuring more success of a planned project.

Keyword Management

Keyword Project Manager allows for the simplified management of thousands of keywords through the use of keyword groups and pools.

Keyword Filters

In order to easily sort through keywords, Keyword Project

Manager provides for 12 keyword filters. Keywords can be sorted and filtered by associated competition data or even keywords within keywords. With a few clicks of a mouse, the user can sort through all of the analysis and information to narrow down his keyword search for the perfect and most potentially profitable keyword.

Import Keywords from Google Adwords Keyword Tool

Creating a list of hundreds of potential keywords using the Google Adwords Keyword Tool is an easy process. These hundreds of keywords and the associated search numbers, adwords competition and CPCs need only be downloaded in CSV (comma separated value) format. Once the list is downloaded, one click will upload it into Keyword Project Manager for analysis and filtering.

Review Results for Keyword Project Manager

Liked:

This reviewer took full advantage of the 7 day, full-featured FREE trial. The only information required is a verifiable email address, although attempts to open multiple accounts for multiple trials using different email addresses is impossible because user IP is recorded. No credit card or payment information is necessary. This respect of information privacy was much appreciated. I did not even need to reveal my name.

Most liked in Keyword Project Manager was the excellent keyword analysis feature. In fact, from a relatively difficult group of keywords, I was able to find a keyword that KPM indicated as "rankable." Using that keyword as the focus of a new project, I did indeed rank on Google's first page in the search results. My position was 6 out of the 10, which was considered to be really good considering the newness of the project.

This reviewer also liked the fact that there is no permanent subscription. One can purchase time as needed, in terms of 1 mo to 1 yr.

There are other features to Keyword Project Manager, such as an SEO article tool where one can compose an SEO article that targets one or more keywords. This feature was played with briefly, not in a serious attempt to compose an article, and it seems to be a great feature if one's gig is to compose SEO content.
Ease in uploading large lists of keywords from Google's keyword tool was also liked. One need only give a name to the group of keywords being uploaded, followed by a one click upload of the file into Keyword Project Manager.

The keyword filters were great for narrowing down the large list of keywords to find one or more keywords that showed promise. One can filter keywords pre or post analysis, or filter only keywords that are not analyzed or analyzed, by multiple criteria. It only requires a few seconds to sort through a massive keyword list to locate the keywords with the specifications desired.

Disliked:

Although the keyword analysis feature of Keyword Project Manager is top-notch, and it should be mentioned that there is no other keyword tool found on the internet that analyzes keywords quite like it, this reviewer disliked how long it took to do the analysis. It takes about 1 minute per keyword to perform the job. During this time, the window must be kept open, although one can continue doing other tasks on his computer by utilizing different tabs or windows. At any rate, when performing keyword analysis on a relatively large list (such as a list prior to filtering), KPM requires a good chunk of time. Noted, though, the results are worth it and to perform the same analysis manually would take even considerably longer.

This reviewer likes the fact that there is no subscription. Usage time can be purchased as needed. However, the minimum amount of time that can be purchased is 1 month. In the course of one month, there is only a limited number of new projects that can be attempted. In effect, much of the time Keyword Project Manager will be idle and not in use by the user. This can lead to paid for "wasted" time. This reviewer has purchased time in addition to the 7 day trial, and though the results when the tool was utilized were worth the investment, I felt one should be able to purchase perhaps 1 day of time when needed. That suggestion has been made to Keyword Project Manager admin.

Conclusion:

It was by mere chance that this reviewer came across Keyword Project Manager on the internet. I was researching a subject related to keywords and the site I visited had an introduction and link to Keyword Project Manager. I thought I would give it a try (considering the free trial, and all) and I am extremely glad that I did. I have seen no other keyword tool, either free or paid, that comes close to performing to the extent of Keyword Project Manager and I foresee that I will need no other keyword tool in the future.

Many times, a keyword researcher will require multiple tools in order to locate keywords that have the most success potential. With Keyword Project Manager, no other tool (aside from the

Google Adwords Keyword tool to initially compile a keyword list and related data) is necessary. Keyword Project Manager gave me all of the information I needed to make effective keyword decisions, and the decisions themselves were simplified because of the data provided with the keyword analysis.

All in all, I found this to be a time-saving keyword tool that out-performs other tools. Well worth the monetary investment necessary to purchase additional time, and well worth the waiting while Keyword Project Manager analyzes the keyword list. If you have not yet tried Keyword Project Manager, it is highly recommended you take advantage of the free trial. You can analyze a lot of keywords in 7 days if you keep Keyword Project Manager working, and then simply download the results for future reference after your trial has expired. I am sure you will be pleased with KPM and will consider purchasing additional time as your keyword research needs demand.

11. Basic Article Format

A basic, quality article has three primary components:

- Introduction
- Body Paragraphs
- Conclusion

In the introduction, the article subject is defined and something along the lines of a hypothesis, premise, approach or objective that the author will meet with the article is stated. The body paragraphs, usually not less than three, logically present the facts that support the hypothesis, premise, approach or objective presented in the introduction. The conclusion simply repeats everything that the reader has been told in the article and makes a final statement as to how the hypothesis, premise, approach or objective was proven.

As a writer becomes more experienced, he will develop his own style of writing. For example, in some circumstances a concluding paragraph may seem unnecessary and the writer will choose not to write one. Article style can be appropriated to the various subjects and situations that the writer comes across during his writing career. For the purpose of adding a little style right from the start, the following features were found to be requested by many individuals and businesses who hire writers to create their content:

- A Bulleted List or Points
- Sub-Headings

When just beginning to write articles, it is a good practice to start becoming accustom to adding a bulleted list or bulleted points. This feature makes an article easier to skim by the reader and generally indicates a better quality, logically presented piece of work.

A bulleted list or points can be placed immediately following the introductory paragraph or elsewhere in the article body as determined to be appropriate. There should be a minimum of 3 points or 3 items to the list, but on occasion less may only be called for. The points or list of items presented should logically be followed up by the body paragraphs that immediately follow the bulleted section. The list can also be related to the sub-headings that the author intends to use in his article format.

Usually, an article of approximately 500 words can have a minimum of 3 hub-headings, separating the different sections of the article. There can be less or more, depending on the article length and the manner in which the article author wants to present his case. Sub-headings are also a feature that people who hire writers seem to request quite often and, again, it makes the article easier to skim by the reader and helps with the logical flow of the article's paragraphs. One or more body paragraphs can be written for each sub-heading.

Generally, sentences and paragraphs should be kept as short as necessary to make their point. This makes the article easier to read. Long, complex sentences should be made into multiple sentences. Paragraphs should be composed of between two and five sentences. Multiple paragraphs should be created if the point being made warrants more sentences.

13. **Writing a Search Engine Optimized Article**

To write a search engine optimized article is not extremely difficult once the writer becomes accustom to writing with keywords. In the beginning, it may be a good idea for the writer to write the article without paying too much attention to the keyword density. After the article is written, the author can go back over the article and insert the necessary keywords in places where they are appropriate, finally insuring that the proper density of the keywords has been met.

The following are general guidelines for keyword placement:

• 	The Primary Keyword should be used in the Article Title.
• 	The Primary Keyword should be used with a density of between 2% and 4% throughout the entire article.
• 	The Primary Keyword should be used in the first sentence of the first paragraph.
• 	In addition to the first sentence, the primary keyword should be used at least one more time in the first paragraph (twice within the first paragraph).
• 	The Primary Keyword should be used in at least one sub-heading.
• 	The Primary Keyword should appear once or

twice in the closing paragraph.

- LSI Keywords should have a total density of about 1%.

By keyword density, it is meant that, depending on the length of the article, the keyword should appear as many times as necessary to make the article word composition equal to a certain percentage. For example, for a 500 word article, the primary keyword should appear 10 to 20 times, making the density 2% to 4%. Do not count the use of the keyword in the title. Do count the use of the keyword in the sub-heading.

For LSI keywords, the total density should be about 1%. LSI keywords need be used only once each up to the number amounting to the density percentage. For example, in a 500 word article, total LSI keyword density should be about 1%. That means a total of approximately 5 LSI keywords should be used once each.

Keywords should be worked into the article where they are appropriate and make sense. An article should not just be keyword stuffed where the keyword placement is out of context or affects the readability of the article.

14. **Sample SEO Lead Hub Article**

Article Title: Mesothelioma Injury: Does it Apply to You?
Primary Keyword: Mesothelioma Injury

Approximately 2,000 new cases relating to mesothelioma injury are diagnosed each year. What this means is that 14 to 30 people out of every million will be diagnosed with asbestos lung cancer in every 12 month period. Mesothelioma injury is primarily caused by exposure to asbestos where particles of the material have been swallowed or inhaled. The period of exposure time does not have to be extraordinary in order to develop malignant mesothelioma.

Mesothelioma Symptoms:

Mesothelioma can be in the process of developing for many years before a victim is alerted by possible signs. Commonly, the disease is discovered when a chest x-ray is taken for reasons that may be unrelated to possible mesothelioma injury. Symptoms of mesothelioma cancer can include:

* Pain in the Abdomen or feelings of "fullness"
* Chest Pain
* Discovering it is Difficult to Swallow
* A Build Up of Fluid in the Lung Linings
* Pain in the Lower Back
* Discovering a Loss of Appetite
* Chronic Coughing
* Experiencing Shortness of Breath
•   General Feelings of Weakness
•

If an individual suspects that he has been exposed to asbestos and recognizes any of the foregoing mesothelioma symptoms, diagnosis by an experienced doctor should be sought to determine if mesothelioma injury applies in his case.

Types of Mesothelioma:

There are 3 primary types of mesothelioma -

* Pleural Mesothelioma
* Pericardial Mesothelioma
* Peritonial Mesothelioma

Pleural mesothelioma is the mesothelioma cancer that is most common, affecting the protective tissues that surround the lungs. Pericardial mesothelioma is the asbestos cancer that affects the tissues that protect the heart. Peritonial mesothelioma is the type of mesothelioma cancer that affects the protective tissues that surround the abdominal lining.

What To Do If You Are Affected by Mesothelioma Injury:

After contacting a doctor and being given a diagnosis of mesothelioma, it may be time to seek out the assistance of a specialized attorney by calling a mesothelioma law firm. A mesothelioma attorney will appropriately represent you and possibly obtain monetary compensation for your suffering by achieving a sizable mesothelioma settlement in your case.

15. Sample SEO Supporting Hub Articles

Article Title: Mesothelioma Settlements: How Much and In How Long
Primary Keyword: Mesothelioma Settlement(s)

Malignant mesothelioma is a rare form of cancer that most often affects people who have been exposed to asbestos. Most commonly, the cancer develops in the lining of the lungs and the internal chest wall. A victim of asbestos exposure who develops mesothelioma cancer will, in most cases, seek monetary damages and hire a mesothelioma law firm to handle his case. By hiring a mesothelioma attorney, a victim can maximize the amount of mesothelioma compensation he receives.

The individual who developed the mesothelioma cancer can be concerned about 2 aspects of his mesothelioma lawsuit:

* What is the amount of mesothelioma lawsuit settlements?
* How long does it take to settle a mesothelioma lawsuit?

Mesothelioma Settlement Amounts:

Mesothelioma settlements can range from a moderate amount of monetary compensation to millions of dollars. Most often, the amount of money received by the victim is related to the cost of medical expenses, the amount of wages that were lost due to the illness and other costs that were incurred or will be incurred as a result of the mesothelioma. The amount of compensation received is also linked to the actual circumstances of individual cases.

In cases where the employing company knowingly exposed the employee to the asbestos material and did not in some way make an effort to protect the employee or disclose the potential danger, ultimate compensation achieved can be in the millions of dollars. The actual amount of many mesothelioma settlement amounts are never revealed to the public, but the court is known to have awarded up to $250 million in one particular case.

How Long Does It Take To Reach Mesothelioma Settlements?

Most mesothelioma lawsuits are settled outside of court, without the case ever going to trial. In a majority of circumstances, the defendant company desires to resolve the claim as quickly and inexpensively as possible. An out-of-court settlement is the fastest way to receive mesothelioma compensation.

Depending on the complexity of the case, there is a chance that an out-of-court settlement will not be the most equitable resolution to the claim. Under these circumstances, mesothelioma lawyers will probably recommend taking the case to trial. A trial takes place usually only after a few settlement offers were made to the defendant and the defendant refused to settle on the offers. A trial, of course, will mandate considerably more time before the victim receives a monetary award. A trial can take months or, sometimes, even longer.

Article Title: When It's Time to Call A
Mesothelioma Law Firm
Primary Keyword: Mesothelioma Law Firm

Mesothelioma is a cancer, usually affecting the lungs and surrounding tissues, that is primarily caused by exposure to asbestos material. Mesothelioma often affects an individual between 10 and 40 years after the exposure has taken place, so the medical standpoint of cases involving people trying to obtain compensation can become quite complicated. If you were diagnosed with mesothelioma and seek money damages, it is time to call an attorney who specializes in mesothelioma lawsuits.

A mesothelioma law firm will first determine who the liable party or parties are. It could be the company that manufactured the asbestos, the company that installed the asbestos, or the company by which the individual was employed when he was imperiled. There is also the possibility that the victim can recover financially from trust funds that were specifically established for mesothelioma victims. Hiring a mesothelioma lawyer which has already won cases representing exposed individuals could make all the difference in whether or not compensation is achieved.

How to Locate a Mesothelioma Law Firm

One of the first questions a mesothelioma victim may struggle with is exactly how to find the best qualified mesothelioma law firm. The following approaches to this dilemma can be taken:

* Check with Former Co-Workers
* Consult a Lawyer's Directory
* Search Online

If you are diagnosed with mesothelioma, the probability is good that people you formerly worked with were also exposed to the danger, were also diagnosed, and have already found a mesothelioma law firm in order to file lawsuits of their own. Some may have already received compensation.

In many cases you can find detailed background information on attorneys who specialize in the mesothelioma lawsuit niche.

Since mesothelioma lawsuits have become big business, many specialty law firms have invested a sizable portion of the profits they have won on internet advertising and websites. Look for in-depth, well-written information. Avoid those advertisements where the attorney appears to boast about all of the money he can easily win for you. You want an attorney who is sensitive to your special needs, not one that will process your case "out of a box". Be investigative and chances are you will be able to narrow your list down to just a few who you can contact to negotiate with.

Selecting the Right Mesothelioma Law Firm for Your Case

After preparing a list of mesothelioma law firms that you feel could best represent you, the next order of action will be to select the right one. First, you should make a telephone inquiry to each of the mesothelioma law firms on your list and schedule an appointment for an initial consultation. During the interview, be sure to find out what you can expect if you decide to have that particular firm handle your case (many of the larger law firms will have written pamphlets prepared for you to take with you for examination); who exactly will be representing you; who you should call if you have questions; and the response time. It is a good indication if the firm states they will respond to you within 24 hours. Also ask for a list of references of clients they have represented in the past who were satisfied with their degree of representation.

The final consideration in your selection of the right mesothelioma law firm for you is the costs and fees involved. Mesothelioma law firms can charge anywhere from 25% to 40% of the amount of compensation they are able to win for you. The key would be to find a quality mesothelioma law firm that will not charge an amount greater than 30% of your recovery. Depending upon the complexity of your specific case, however, you may choose to hire the law firm with the best experience and track-record in the handling of similar cases, even if their fee is slightly higher. Be sure you feel comfortable with the mesothelioma law firm you decide upon and that you can communicate clearly with it.

How You Can Assist The Law Firm that Represents You

When it's time to call a mesothelioma law firm, you should understand that the law firm will take care of the majority of work involved in your case. However, there are steps you can take to positively assist the attorneys and that may be required by the procedure.

* Gather All of Your Medical Information
* Put Together a Work History
* Record All of Your Out-of-Pocket Expenses

Gathering all of your medical information would include exactly when you were diagnosed and the names and contact information of all of your attending physicians. You may be required to provide detailed medical records relating to your treatments.

By providing a detailed work history, the attorney will be able to more easily determine who may be liable in your case and also prove that you were indeed a victim of asbestos exposure.

Recording all of your Out-of-Pocket expenses would include the costs expended for doctors, hospitals, necessary tests, prescribed medications and possible medical equipment you required due to your illness. These amounts can be included in the monetary damages you are seeking. Report these amounts to your mesothelioma law firm in order that you receive adequate remuneration.

How much time will pass before a mesothelioma settlement in your case is reached will depend upon how complicated your specific lawsuit is. This can be several months. During that time, remember that your mesothelioma law firm is there to help you, so do not be cautious about asking questions. You may also want to keep your own notes and records as the case progresses so that you will not forget important things that may develop. Also, a good mesothelioma law firm will understand the difficulties you and your family have or may experience as a result of your illness. So do not partake in the litigation more than you feel you are able or if you need time to focus mainly on your treatment and spend time with friends and relatives.

When it is time to call a mesothelioma law firm, if because of your illness you are not feeling up to par, you should seek the assistance of people close to you to help you in finding the most qualified legal help and for the support and encouragement you may need to see you through the entire process. You may experience times that may cause you mental anguish. In addition to your loved ones, a mesothelioma law firm can be the key to you recovering the compensation you deserve for your suffering.

16. Using a Video to Enhance Search Engine Optimization

The use of videos to help an article or website rank in the search results is a technique that has been successful time and again. Videos are much easier to rank than static pages. By embedding an optimized video, one that will usually achieve a rank position usually within 30 minutes of upload, an important link is shared by the video and the static page one wants to rank.

The page rank 9 link (YouTube has a page rank of 9) enhances the optimization of the static page, helping it to achieve a higher rank than without the video. In addition, YouTube is the second largest search engine in the world, so the link of the static page in the video description can encourage additional organic traffic.

17. Creating a Video for YouTube

Creating a video, that will ultimately be embedded on the lead hub, requires about 30 minutes of time. The following are necessary:

- A YouTube Account
- Microsoft Powerpoint Software
- Powerpoint to AVI Video Conversion Software
- Royalty Free Music that can be used

Commercially
- Images (optional) that can be used with permission Commercially

Opening a YouTube account is free. Microsoft Powerpoint software comes with the Microsoft Office suite, which most people own. It is a popular software that can be purchased at any office supply store. The Powerpoint to AVI video conversion software is a free download. The powerpoint conversion software from E.M. Can be downloaded using the following link to the EffectMatrix site:

http://www.effectmatrix.com/PowerPoint-Video-Converter/Free-PowerPoint-Video-Converter.htm

Royalty free music that can be used to add a soundtrack to the powerpoint conversion video can be obtained free of charge at the following site:

http://www.music4yourvids.co.uk

Free images that can be used commercially can be obtained at the pixabay site:

http://www.pixabay.com

First, create a powerpoint slide presentation. Use the "title slide" format on all of the slides. Do not be overly wordy with each slide. Each slide should be able to be casually read in about 5 seconds. You can break longer sentences into multiple slides. The "article" used to create the powerpoint presentation can be simply a brief summary of the lead hub article, mentioning key points, since the video will be embedded on the lead hub. Images can be added or used as the background on various slides.

The powerpoint should be created so that it does not consist of more than 35 slides, including the "credits" slide. When converted, each slide will visible for 6 seconds. The entire video does not need to be longer than 1.5 to 2 minutes, but can be longer if so desired. The final slide should be the "credits" slide, which is absolutely necessary. It should read as follows:

Free Commercial Use Images from:
Pixabay.com

Free Commercial Use Music from:
Music4yourvids.co.uk

When the slides are completed, run them in presentation/slideshow mode within the powerpoint software in order to review the work. Once satisfied with the slideshow appearance, it can be converted into a video. Be sure to save the work as a powerpoint presentation.

Open the E.M. Powerpoint to Video conversion software program. The objective is to convert the powerpoint presentation to an AVI video with music. The software is easy to use. The music track intended for use should be downloaded and in a file on the same computer.

The powerpoint presentation file must be uploaded/selected into the software. Then the selection of AVI video must be made. Prior to starting the conversion process, be sure to indicate/upload the music file in the audio selection section. Then convert the file. The entire process takes a few minutes and the completed AVI file will be stored on the computer in the folder indicated by the conversion software. The target folder can be adjusted to any folder selected by the user.

Locate the AVI file on the computer and double-click. The file should open in the computer's media reading program so that the finished video can be viewed. Once satisfied with the viewing, the AVI file can be uploaded to YouTube.

18. Optimization Technique for the Video

The keyword list for the lead hub should be handy in order to optimize the video, targeting the same keywords. The following is a general guideline for video SEO:

- Use the Primary Keyword in the Video Title. The video can have the same title as the lead hub.
- In the video description, put the link to the lead

hub first.

- Following the lead hub link, list the keywords. List the primary keyword first, followed by the LSI keywords on the list. This can be done in paragraph format provided the keywords are comma separated.
- On the computer's clipboard, copy the comma separated keyword "paragraph" (without the hub link).
- Paste the keyword "paragraph" once again further down the description page (an "article" will be written between the 2 keyword "paragraphs").
- Paste the keyword "paragraph" into the "tags" section.
- Write a few paragraphs between the two keyword "paragraphs", making use of the primary keyword (use several times) and the LSI keywords (approximately 5).
- The few paragraphs that are written should be related to the video, perhaps another summary of the lead hub article (but do not use any verbatim sections of the lead hub article – it will appear as duplicate content and be rejected by HubPages).
- Select the most appropriate category for the video.
- Select "standard" YouTube license.
- Be sure to save all changes.
- From the "video manager", click on the video to view it.

- "Like" your own video.
- Click on the "share" link. The "embed" code must be copied and ultimately pasted into position on the lead hub.

19. **Putting the HubPages Project Together**

- Write the Supporting Hub Articles first, armed with the appropriate keyword lists.
- Link the two supporting hubs to each other. Somewhere in each article, embed the primary keyword for the other. "Select" the keyword and create a link to the hub the keyword belongs to.
- Commercial use images that are related to the articles can be upload to the appropriate hub capsule from pixabay.com.
- Write the lead hub.
- Upload an appropriate image from pixabay.com for the lead hub.
- Create the lead hub video and optimize it.
- Paste the "embed" code from the video into a "video" capsule that has been positioned above the text and image (at the very top) on the lead hub.
- Somewhere within the lead hub text, embed the primary keywords for the two supporting hubs. Using the keywords, create links back to

the supporting hubs individually (the keyword link will lead to the supporting hub the keyword belongs to).

- Optionally, monetize your hubs with Amazon and eBay products.
- Publish the Hubs. Hubs can be saved in unpublished format while they are being worked on and until they are completely ready for publication.
- Quality Assessment by HubPages will take approximately 24 hours. Then the project will be live.

20. **Resources**

HubPages Sign-up: http://tinyurl.com/yupperhub
Keyword Project Manager:
http://tinyurl.com/yupperkpm
Powerpoint to AVI Conversion Software:

http://www.effectmatrix.com/PowerPoint-Video-Converter/Free-PowerPoint-Video-Converter.htm

Commercial Use Free Music:
http://www.music4yourvids.co.uk
Commercial Use Free Images:
http://www.pixabay.com

www.ingramcontent.com/pod-product-compliance
Lightning Source LLC
Chambersburg PA
CBHW070504290526
45790CB00003B/1087